Plenty Good Room

A BIBLE STUDY BASED ON AFRICAN AMERICAN SPIRITUALS

TAMARA E. LEWIS

Abingdon Press / Nashville

PLENTY GOOD ROOM: A BIBLE STUDY BASED ON AFRICAN AMERICAN SPIRITUALS
LEADER BOOK AND CD

This book is printed on acid-free, elemental-chlorine-free paper.

Library of Congress Cataloging-in-Publication Data

ISBN 0-687-05034-0

02 03 04 05 06 07 08 09 10 11 — 10 9 8 7 6 5 4 3 2 1

MANUFACTURED IN THE UNITED STATES OF AMERICA

Contents

Preparing to Lead the Study 4

Teaching and Learning Guidelines 4

Session One:
"Rock-a My Soul" 5

Session Two:
"Go Down, Moses" 7

Session Three:
"Balm in Gilead" 9

Session Four:
"Ain't Dat Good News?" 11

Session Five:
"Every Time I Feel the Spirit" 13

Session Six:
"Plenty Good Room" 15

Preparing to Lead the Study

African American spirituals are among the most beautiful contributions to the world of sacred music. Their infectious melodies, harmonies, textures, and rhythms make this genre distinctive and enriching.

In preparing to lead the study, reflect on your own familiarity with the six spirituals. In what settings have you heard them? Take time to listen to the spirituals on the CD. How do the songs make you feel? Is the biblical theme of each spiritual clear to you? Imagine what the slaves might have been thinking while singing or hearing one of these songs. Spending time alone listening to the sound, message, and emotions of the spirituals will help you in your leadership of the group.

Reflect on your understanding and impressions of slavery in America. What feelings come to mind when you think of that time? What do you believe about God's interaction in the affairs of human history? How is God active and working in today's world? Are you the descendants of slaves or slave owners? How does this knowledge affect you when thinking about this subject? Pray and meditate on these themes, and write down any issues or concerns.

Teaching and Learning Guidelines

Plenty Good Room is organized around stories. Study the stories in the sessions, have participants tell their own stories, or find additional stories while concentrating on the Scripture,

Each session is divided into four parts. The first part describes the unique musical sound and emotional impact of each spiritual. The second part offers historical background, stories and anecdotes about discusses the settings in which spirituals originated, and the socio-political ramifications of the lyrics. The third part features Scripture passages that form the basis of each spiritual. The fourth part helps participants apply the understandings of the past to the contemporary world.

Many persons may find the issues raised in this study to be sensitive. Encourage an atmosphere of mutual trust and congeniality. Help participants to remember that the goal of this study is simply to be open to more meaningful relationships with each other and with God, as well as to promote reconciliation and healing.

Create an environment conducive to learning. Place before the group an item or two that relates thematically to the study, such as musical symbols, African art, or historical photos. During discussions, try to ask probing, insightful questions. Include both thoughts and feelings. Keep the lines of communication open. Practice positive affirmations.

4

SESSION ONE

Luke 16:19-26

Key verse: "But Abraham said, 'Child remember that during your life-
time you received your good things, and Lazarus in like
manner evil things; but now he is comforted here, and you
are in agony'" (Luke 16:25).

"Rock-a My Soul"

Chorus:
Rock-a my soul in the bosom of Abraham
Rock-a my soul in the bosom of Abraham
Rock-a my soul in the bosom of Abraham
Oh, rock-a my soul

Rock-a my soul in the bosom of Abraham
Rock-a my soul in the bosom of Abraham
Rock-a my soul in the bosom of Abraham
Oh, rock-a my soul

Verse:
So high, you can't get over it
So low, you can't get under it
So wide, you can't get around it
Oh, rock-a my soul

Chorus:
Rock-a my soul in the bosom of Abraham
Rock-a my soul in the bosom of Abraham
Rock-a my soul in the bosom of Abraham
Oh, rock-a my soul (Repeat Verse)

Session Outline

Opening (10-15 minutes)

Play "Rock-a My Soul" as participants enter the room. (Most CD players
have a repeat function that allows for a song to play over and over.)
Welcome participants and lead them in an opening prayer. Allow participants to introduce themselves and to express why they are interested in this
study. Have an opening discussion about general impressions of African
American spirituals, especially "Rock-a My Soul" and its biblical content.

5

Music (10-15 minutes)

Have participants read aloud "Holy Movement and Worship," pages 9-10 in the student book. Then listen to "Rock-a My Soul" again. Ask: Do you agree with the musical description of this spiritual? What would you change about the description to more adequately reflect the way the spiritual sounds? How does the music affect your feelings, influence your thoughts, enhance your praise and worship? Ask participants if they know any stories associated with the song or if they have personal anecdotes or testimonies in their experience with the spiritual.

Setting and Context (15-20 minutes)

Ask different persons to take turns reading "Rock of One's Soul," pages 10-11 in the student book. Discuss the following questions: Why do you think the authors of the spirituals are anonymous? What do you think it was like to have to gather secretly to worship? What did the brush harbor environment do for worship? Would having to worship secretly or praising aloud using code words strengthen or diminish your faith?

Scripture Passage (15-20 minutes)

Have participants form small groups of two or three. Assign each group to read "A Parable by Jesus," page 12 and "Origin and Destiny of Our Souls," page 13. Then ask the groups to reflect on the questions in the Food for Thought section on page 13. Give the groups ten to fifteen minutes to think of as many ideas as they can. Have participants reassemble and discuss their answers to the questions asked in their groups.

Reflection and Closing (10-15 minutes)

Play "Rock-a My Soul" again, asking participants to sing along. Invite the participants to stand and to clap their hands. As they sing, ask them to imagine how the slaves would have sung the song together and how they would have been affected by the song's message.

After the song, ask participants to reflect on the song and the session. They may describe how they were impressed by the biblical connection to the spiritual. There may be other insights into the historical context and the musical sounds and rhythms of the song. Have someone lead the group in a closing prayer.

SESSION TWO

Exodus 3:1-10

Key verse: "Then the LORD said, 'I have observed the misery of my people who are in Egypt; I have heard their cry on account of their taskmasters. Indeed, I know their sufferings'" (Exodus 3:7).

"Go Down, Moses"

Verse:
When Israel was in Egypt land:
Let my people go;
Oppressed so hard they could not stand,
Let my people go.

Chorus:
Go down, Moses,
'Way down in Egypt land,
Tell ole Pharaoh,
To let my people go.

Verse:
"Thus saith the Lord," bold Moses said,
Let my people go;
"If not, I'll smite your first-born dead,"
Let my people go. (Repeat Chorus)

Verse:
No more shall they in bondage toil,
Let my people go;
Let them come out with Egypt's spoil,
Let my people go. (Repeat Chorus)

Session Outline

Opening (15-20 minutes)

Welcome participants. Play "Go Down, Moses." Have someone read "Heart and Soul," pages 14-15 in the student book. If there are participants present who did not study Session One, play "Rock-a My Soul." Then ask participants to compare their impressions of "Rock-a My Soul" with "Go Down, Moses." Ask: What are the differences in sound, emotions, and feel-

7

ings evoked from listening to the two spirituals? How do you think the musical expression of these two spirituals reflects the different attitudes of slaves in the course of their experience?

Have participants name the specific feelings engendered when listening to "Go Down, Moses." Faith, strength, hope, fear, pain? Discuss why certain emotions are felt when hearing a particular song.

Setting, Bible, and Context (20-25 minutes)

Ask someone to read aloud Exodus 3:1-10. Have participants read "Escape and Deliverance From Slavery," pages 15-16 and "Quest for Freedom," page 16. Discuss the following questions: How does "Go Down, Moses" indicate what the slaves thought about being in slavery? What do you know about the Underground Railroad and well-known "conductors," such as Harriet Tubman? What do the stories of heroic persons who fought against slavery indicate about God's will and purpose for humanity? How does "Go Down, Moses" reflect the way the slaves would have interpreted the Exodus passage?

Reflection (20-25 minutes)

Form small groups of two or three. Have participants in each group read silently "Justice and Equality" on page 18. Ask the groups to discuss the questions in the Food for Thought section on page 19. Then ask participants to reassemble to discuss their answers to the questions discussed.

Encourage participants to think about the topic of slavery from a political and economic standpoint. Have them note specifically (1) the enslavement of the Israelites by the Egyptians and (2) the history of American slavery. What were the political and social rights of the Israelites? How did their work benefit the Egyptian state? What made slavery so profitable in the United States?

Ask participants if they know about systems of slavery that exist today in places such as the Sudan and parts of the Arab world. Discuss how Christians can help slaves today. What are other instances of global oppression? How do terrorist conflicts and attacks relate to global oppression? What other oppressive forces are present in our world? How can an understanding of spirituals like "Go Down, Moses" inspire Christians to struggle for change?

Closing

Play "Go Down, Moses" again, inviting participants to sing. At the conclusion of the song, or while the song is playing at a lowered volume, have someone lead the class in a closing prayer.

SESSION THREE

Jeremiah 8:18-22

Key verse: "Is there no balm in Gilead? / Is there no physician there? / Why then has the health of my poor people / not been restored?" (Jeremiah 8:22).

"Balm in Gilead"

Chorus:
There is a balm in Gilead,
To make the wounded whole,
There is a balm in Gilead,
To heal the sin-sick soul.

Verse:
Sometimes I feel discouraged,
And think my work's in vain,
But then the Holy Spirit
Revives my soul again.
(Repeat Chorus)

Verse:
Don't ever feel discouraged,
For Jesus is your friend,
And if you look for knowledge,
He'll ne'er refuse to lend.
(Repeat Chorus)

Verse:
If you cannot preach like Peter,
If you cannot pray like Paul
You can tell the love of Jesus,
And say "He died for all."
(Repeat Chorus)

Session Outline

Opening (10-15 minutes)

Play "Balm in Gilead" as participants enter. Ask them to listen to the song at least once, reflecting silently on the words and music. Have someone read "Plaintive and Soothing Harmony," pages 20-21 in the student book.

9

Discuss the impression the spirituals make on the listeners. How does the impression compare with the musical description of the song? What emotions surface while listening to "Balm in Gilead"? What additional terms could be used to describe the song?

Historical Setting (15-20 minutes)

Ask two or more persons to take turns reading "Slavery's Balm for Weary Souls" on pages 21-23.

Ask: What is your perception of this section? Do you agree or disagree with the way slavery is described? Why? How do some of the personal testimonies by former slaves affect the ways in which you think about slavery? Are you surprised by some of the stories? Why or why not? What personal stories or anecdotes would you like to share? What does it mean to you to know that many slaves were inspired to survive through the Christian faith?

Scripture Passage (20-30 minutes)

Form groups of two or three and ask each group to read Jeremiah 8:14-22 and discuss the text, concentrating on the poetry, rhythm, and feel of the words. Have the groups read "Jeremiah's Cry," pages 23-24 and "There Is a Balm," page 25.

When the participants reassemble, invite them to compare the words of the spiritual with Jeremiah's words. Ask: In the biblical text, who is the speaker? God? a prophet? the people? the congregation? Encourage each group to compare Jeremiah's setting, understanding of God, and interpretation of the people's pain with the situation of the slaves. How are they different? How are they the same? Is there a commonality in the sense of suffering of the two groups of people? Why or why not?

Jeremiah views the Israelites as being responsible for their suffering due to not following God. Does this relate in any way to the slaves' situation? Why or why not? How does "Balm in Gilead" address suffering? How were the slaves able to have such hope in the face of overwhelming odds?

Reflection and Closing (15-20 minutes)

Ask someone to read aloud "Carrying the Balm's Mantle" on pages 25-26. Have participants respond to the questions in the Food for Thought section on page 26. Some of these questions may have already been addressed by previous discussions. Ask participants if they feel an urgent call to act in today's world by comforting the sick, helping the homeless, or fighting for justice. Play "Balm in Gilead" again. Invite everyone to stand, to join hands, and to sing the spiritual together as a closing benediction.

SESSION FOUR

Mark 8:34-35

Key verse: "For those who want to save their life will lose it, and those who lose their life for my sake, and for the sake of the gospel will save it" (Mark 8:35).

"Ain't Dat Good News?"

Verse:
Got a crown up in-a dat Kingdom,
Ain't-a dat good news?
Got a crown up in-a dat Kingdom,
Ain't-a dat good news?

Chorus:
I'm a-gonna lay down dis world,
Gonna shoulder up my cross,
Gonna take it home-a to my Jesus,
Ain't-a dat good news?

Verse:
Got a harp up in-a dat Kingdom . . .
    (Repeat Chorus)
Got a robe up in-a dat Kingdom . . .
    (Repeat Chorus)

Verse:
Got slippers in-a dat Kingdom . . .
    (Repeat Chorus)
Got a Savior in-a dat Kingdom . . .
    (Repeat Chorus)

Session Outline

Opening (10-15 minutes)

Welcome participants as "Ain't Dat Good News?" plays. Lead the class in an opening prayer. Review the spirituals studied so far. Ask: Which spirituals do you like the most? The least? Why? What do you remember most about the biblical and spiritual themes of the songs? What do you remember about the historical context and setting of the slaves? Allow time for participants to offer any new thoughts they may have since the last session. Invite them to give personal testimonies or revelations they have experienced since beginning the study.

Music and Context (15-20 minutes)

Let "Ain't Dat Good News?" play softly in the background as participants take turns reading aloud "Joyous Musical Expression," pages 27-28 and "Mighty Good News?" on pages 28-29 of the student book. Discuss how the lack of physical comfort and basic material goods may have affected the words of "Ain't Dat Good News?" Ask: How can the words be interpreted in contemporary ways? How does the happy, rhythmic sway of the music influence the words that are sung? Does the music encourage particular feelings or emotions? If so, what are they? Does the music sound contemporary or old-fashioned? Is this a good song for praise and worship? Why or why not?

Scripture Passage (15-20 minutes)

Have someone read aloud Mark 8:34-36, then ask participants to read silently "Crowns in the Kingdom," pages 30-31 and "Taking Up Our Crosses," pages 31-32. Discuss the themes of the song, the Scripture passage, and the setting of the slaves. Ask: What are the issues (the condition of the slaves? Bible testimony? a theological understanding of heaven?)? How did the slaves literally interpret death and salvation? How do the lyrics of "Ain't Dat Good News?" answer the slaves' interpretation of death and salvation? What might be missing from the spiritual that would help us understand the slaves' interpretation?

Slaves were not a homogenous group and surely must have had different interpretations of suffering and heaven. What could some of those varying perspectives have been? What different views of heaven does the contemporary Christian community have?

Reflection (10-15 minutes)

Form small groups of two or three, and ask each group to answer the questions in the Food for Thought section on page 32. Have the participants to reassemble and discuss their answers.

Closing (5 minutes)

Lead the group in singing "Ain't Dat Good News?" or have participants read the lyrics aloud. Allow time for prayer requests, and have someone lead the group in a closing prayer.

SESSION FIVE

Acts 2:1-4

Key verse: "**All of them were filled with the Holy Spirit and began to speak in other languages, as the Spirit gave them ability**" **(Acts 2:4).**

"Every Time I Feel the Spirit"

Chorus:
Every time I feel the Spirit
Moving in my heart, I will pray.
Yes, every time I feel the Spirit
Moving in my heart, I will pray.

Verse:
Upon the mountain my Lord spoke,
Out of His mouth came fire and smoke.
Looked all around me, it looked so shine,
Till I asked my Lord if all was mine.

Every time I feel the Spirit
Moving in my heart, I will pray.
Yes, every time I feel the Spirit
Moving in my heart, I will pray.

Verse:
Jordan River is chilly and cold,
It chills the body but not the soul.
There ain't but one train on this track,
Runs to heaven and right back.
(Repeat Chorus)

Session Outline

Opening (5-10 minutes)

Play "Every Time I Feel the Spirit" as participants gather. Urge them to begin singing, clapping, and waving their hands to the music. "Every Time I Feel the Spirit" is an extremely happy, upbeat spiritual, emphasizing a deep sense of joy and anticipation. Encourage the group to enjoy the music, taking the opportunity to praise and worship God. During this time, participants may find themselves bonding in Christian unity through communal worship. Invite them to "let go" and praise the Lord!

Music and Context (20-25 minutes)

Read aloud "Lively Celebration," pages 33-34 in the student book. Then ask: Do you agree with the description of the song? Why or why not? How does the song reflect your experience of praise and worship? Is "Every Time I Feel the Spirit" a good praise and worship song? Why or why not? In what worship settings would this song affect the level of praise?

Have participants read "Prayer and Slavery," pages 34-36. Ask: What is the connection, if any, between prayer and singing? How could singing be considered a kind of prayer? How has the power of prayer affected your life? How might the act of prayer have strengthened the slaves' sense of well-being? Do you believe that the slaves' prayers eventually helped to free them? Why or why not?

In regard to the slaves who died before they were made free, as well as those who continued to suffer after slavery, do you think God heard their prayers? Why or why not? Have you experienced a "call and response" prayer, one in which the leader prays and the congregation responds? Is this a common method of prayer in your church? If so, is it particularly meaningful to you? If not, what did you think about the experience? Have you felt the Spirit of God move within as you prayed? If so, what was that experience like? How do you describe the Holy Spirit?

Scripture Passage (20-25 minutes)

Form smaller groups of two or three, and have them read aloud Acts 2:1-4. Ask the groups to read "The Holy Spirit Comes," pages 36-37 and "Pentecost as Empowerment," page 37. When participants have reassembled, discuss the questions in the Food for Thought section on page 38. Invite participants to give Bible verses, prayers, or spiritual themes that have been particularly meaningful to them.

Closing (10-15 minutes)

Play "Every Time I Feel the Spirit" again. Ask the participants to gather in a circle.

Ask participants to concentrate on the loving power of God in their hearts. Have them imagine that they have gathered to praise and worship God despite the terrible conditions of slavery. Have them sing along with the spiritual, clapping their hands and singing praises to God. As the song ends, have someone lead the class in a closing prayer.

SESSION SIX

Key verse: "In my Father's house there are many dwelling places. If it were not so, would I have told you that I go to prepare a place for you?" (John 14:2).

John 14:1-4

"Plenty Good Room"

Chorus:
There's plenty good room, plenty good room,
Plenty good room in my Father's kingdom,
Plenty good room, plenty good room,
Just choose your seat and sit down!

Verse:
I would not be a sinner,
I'll tell you the reason why;
I'm afraid my Lord might call on me,
And I wouldn't be ready to die.

There's plenty good room, plenty good room,
Plenty good room in my Father's kingdom,
Plenty good room, plenty good room,
Just choose your seat and sit down!

Verse:
I would not be a liar,
I'll tell you the reason why;
I'm afraid my Lord might call on me,
And I wouldn't be ready to die. (Repeat chorus)

Sit down! Sit down! Sit down!

Session Outline

Opening Session (10-15 minutes)

Welcome participants quietly as they enter. Do not play any music during this time. Announce that this is the last session of the study. Thank everyone for sharing the experience with you and offer your insights in leading and participating with the group. Talk about which spirituals you have enjoyed the most and what themes have resonated with your faith.

Then ask participants to take turns saying only one word to describe the lives of the slaves. Before playing "Plenty Good Room," ask participants to listen to the song without speaking. After the song has played, ask: What word comes to mind when you hear this spiritual? (This exercise allows participants to think deliberately about their understanding of slavery and of this particular spiritual.)

Music and Context (10-15 minutes)

Play "Plenty Good Room" again. Allow participants to take turns reading the paragraphs in "Heaven Is a Place," pages 39-40 and "Judgment and Death" on pages 40-41. Ask: Why do you think the slaves clung to the idea of heaven? Do contemporary Christians share such a literal view of heaven? What do you think about the slaves' looking forward to death? What are your ideas of heaven? Do you see it as a physical place? How would you describe it? How does the sound of the music imply that the song is talking about heaven? What do you think are the moral prescriptions for entering heaven? How does this song interpret the lifestyle necessary for entering heaven? What are the contemporary Christian views of sin, grace, and salvation? How do these views vary among denominations, groups, or individuals? How can we be affected by the witness of the faith and beliefs evidenced in the spirituals?

Reflection (20-25 minutes)

Have participants form small groups, and ask them to read "Standing on the Shoulders of Giants," page 42. Invite the groups to respond to questions in the Food for Thought section on page 44.

Closing (25-30 minutes)

Ask participants to form a circle. Invite them to share what insights they gained from the group discussions and how they interpret *Plenty Good Room*. Ask participants to offer their reflections on the entire study if they wish, what they liked about it, what could have been better, and what they learned, for example.

Play all six spirituals, allowing participants to sing and worship or to listen reflectively. Lead the group in a circle prayer or have persons make known their prayer requests. Ask participants to choose one of the spirituals that they would like to sing together. Encourage them to sing with faith, reverence, and devotion as a closing benediction.